PIANO
VOCAL
GUITAR

2   Zoo Station

11   Even Better Than the Real Thing

18   One

25   Until the End of the World

34   Who's Gonna Ride Your Wild Horses

43   So Cruel

55   The Fly

64   Mysterious Ways

71   Tryin' to Throw Your Arms Around

79   Ultraviolet (Light My Way)

89   Acrobat

100   Love Is Blindness

ISBN 978-1-4584-2146-3

HAL•LEONARD®
CORPORATION
7777 W. BLUEMOUND RD. P.O. BOX 13819 MILWAUKEE, WI 53213

Visit Hal Leonard Online at
www.halleonard.com

ZOO STATION

Lyrics by BONO and THE EDGE
Music by U2

Zoo Sta - tion.

EVEN BETTER THAN THE REAL THING

Lyrics by BONO and THE EDGE
Music by U2

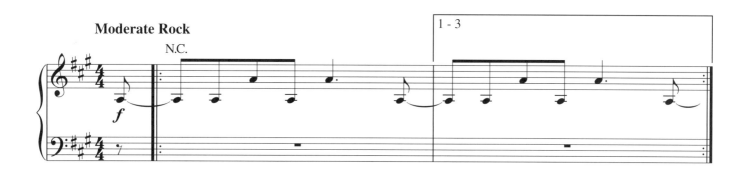

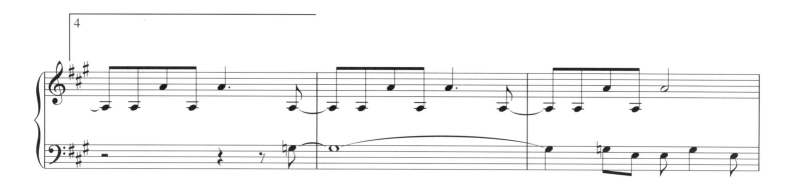

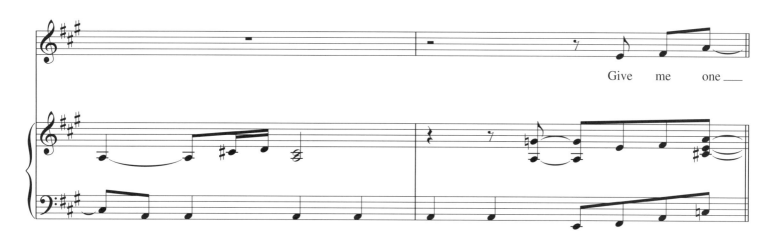

Give me one ___

14

ONE

Lyrics by BONO and THE EDGE
Music by U2

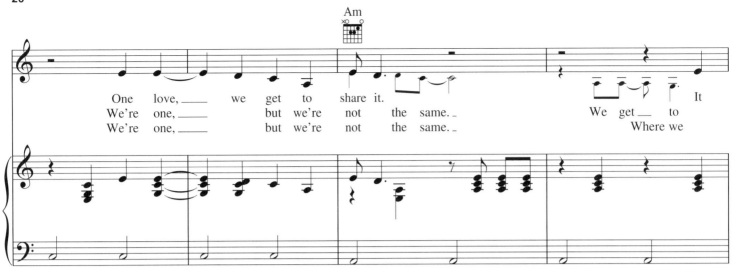

One love, ___ we get to share it.
We're one, ___ but we're not the same. _
We're one, ___ but we're not the same. _ It
We get ___ to
Where we

leaves you, ba - by, if you don't care for it. ___
car - ry each oth - er, car - ry each oth - er.
hurt each oth - er, and we're do - in' it a - gain.

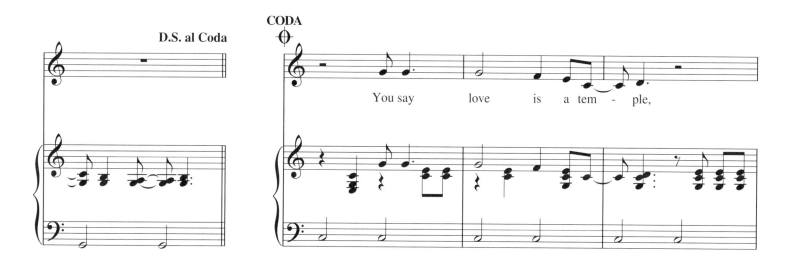

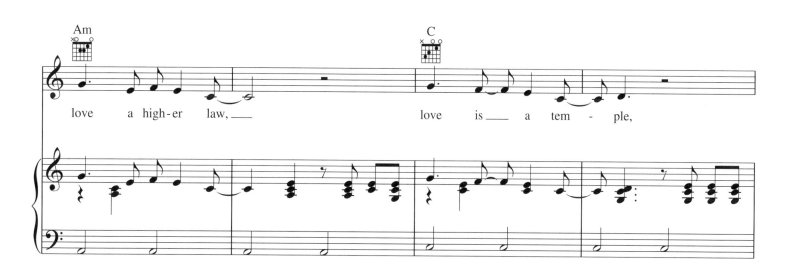

UNTIL THE END OF THE WORLD

Lyrics by BONO and THE EDGE
Music by U2

Moderately

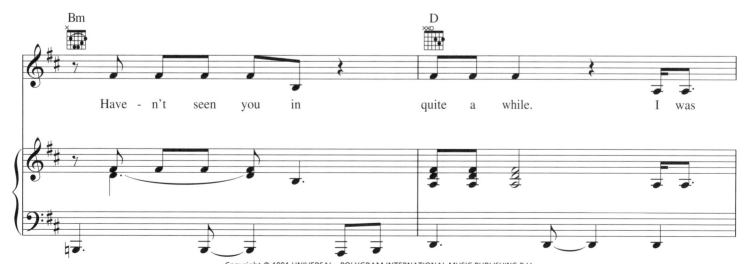

Have - n't seen you in   quite a   while.   I was

Waves of re-gret and waves of joy. ____ I reached out ____ for the one ____ I tried to de-stroy. ____ You, ____ you said you'd wait ____ 'til the end of the world. ____

Play 4 times

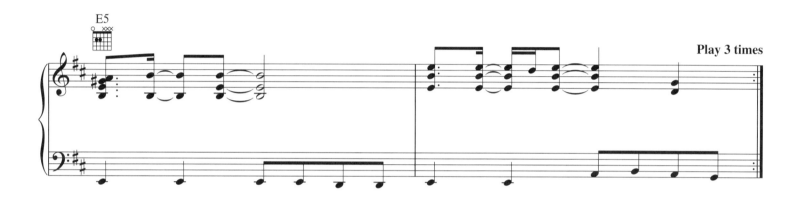

WHO'S GONNA RIDE YOUR WILD HORSES

Lyrics by BONO and THE EDGE
Music by U2

Moderately fast

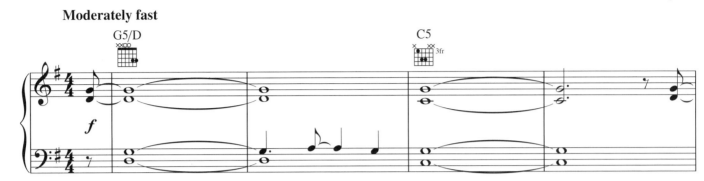

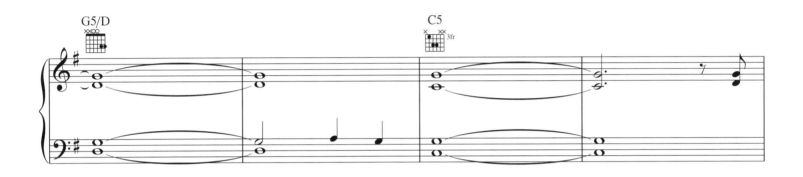

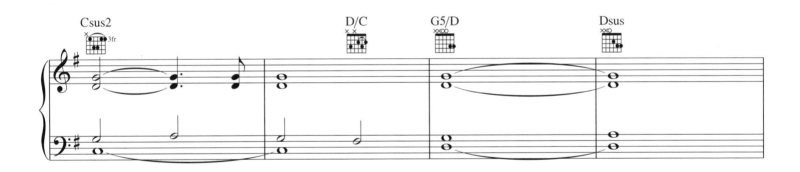

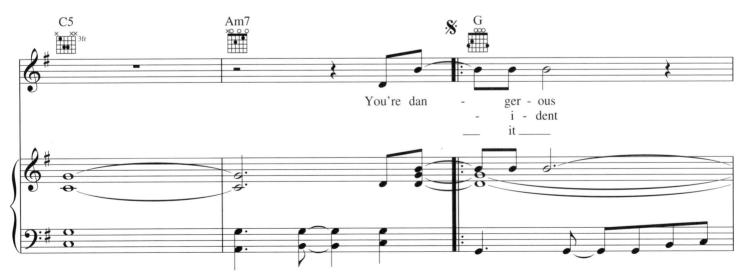

You're dan - ger - ous
- i - dent
__ it ____

SO CRUEL

Lyrics by BONO and THE EDGE
Music by U2

THE FLY

Lyrics by BONO and THE EDGE
Music by U2

Moderately fast

N.C.

(Spoken:) Oh, baby child.   *(Sung:)* It's   no

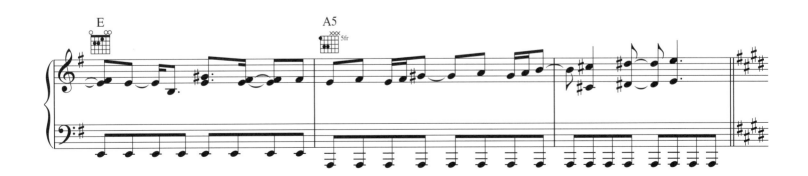

(Love, _____ we shine like a burn - ing star. __ We're fall -

- ing from __ the sky _____
(2nd time only) A man will __ rise, _____ a man will __ fall __

__ to - night.) _____
__ from the sheer face _ of

one man's lie. ___ Look, I've got-ta go. Yeah, I'm run-ning out of change. There's a

lot of things ___ if ___ I could, I'd re - ar - range. ___

rit.

MYSTERIOUS WAYS

Lyrics by BONO and THE EDGE
Music by U2

Johnny take a walk with your sister the moon. Let her pale light in to
Johnny take a dive with your sister in the rain. Let her talk about the things you

fill up your room. You've been living underground, eating from a can. You've been
can't explain. To touch is to heal. To hurt is to steal. If you

65

It's al - right, __ it's al - right, __ it's al - right.

Lift my days, light up my nights, ___ oh.

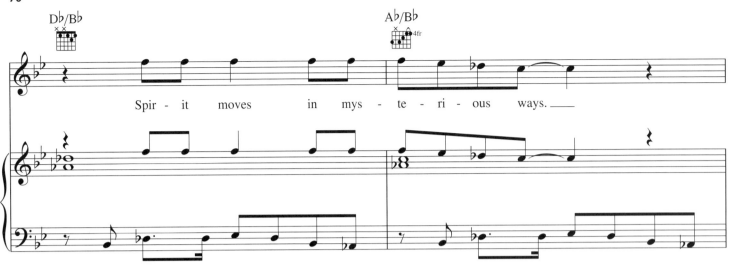

Spir- it moves in mys- te- ri- ous ways. ___

She moves ___ with it.   She moves ___ with it.

Lift my days and light up my nights, ___ oh.

TRYIN' TO THROW YOUR ARMS AROUND

Lyrics by BONO and THE EDGE
Music by U2

Six o'-clock in the morn-ing, you're the last to hear the warn-ing; } you've been
Sun-rise like a nose-bleed, well, your head hurts and you can't breathe; } you've been

try-in' to throw your arms a-round the world.

{ You've been

ULTRAVIOLET
(Light My Way)

Lyrics by BONO and THE EDGE
Music by U2

ACROBAT

Lyrics by BONO and THE EDGE
Music by U2

Moderately, in 1

Play 4 times

Don't _ be - lieve what you hear;
No, ___ noth - ing makes sense.

don't be - lieve ___ what you see.
Noth - ing ___ seems to see. / fit.

If you ___ just ___ close your eyes, you can ___
I know ___ you'd hit out, if you ___

house, and ev - 'ry book has ___ been ___ read. ___

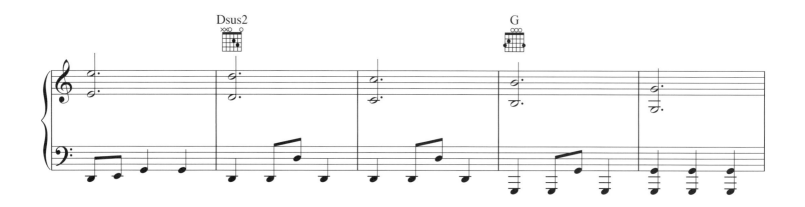

but I know _____ that the tide is turn - ing _____ 'round. _____

So don't let _____ the bas - tards _____ grind you down. ___

LOVE IS BLINDNESS

Lyrics by BONO and THE EDGE
Music by U2

Love is